The
Magician
of Auschwitz

Written by Kathy Kacer
Illustrated by Gillian Newland

Second Story Press

Acknowledgments

I am indebted to the wonderful people who support and promote my writing. Margie Wolfe, publisher extraordinaire, along with Kathryn Cole, Melissa Kaita, Emma Rodgers, and Phuong Truong. Many thanks to Gillian Newland for the stunning illustrations.

I'm grateful to John Freund for introducing me to the story of Nivelli the Magician, and for leading me to Werner Reich. I knew I wanted to write this book as soon as I met Werner. He is strong, articulate, passionate, and funny. Many thanks to Werner and his wonderful wife, Eva, for generously opening their home on Long Island to me.

Thank you to my wonderful friends and family for all the laughter and strength. And as always to my husband, Ian Epstein, and my children, Gabi Epstein and Jake Epstein—the loves of my life!

Dedication
To Werner and Eva Reich, with love and admiration

LIBRARY AND ARCHIVES CANADA CATALOGUING IN PUBLICATION

Kacer, Kathy, 1954-, author
The magician of Auschwitz / by Kathy Kacer ; illustrated by Gillian Newland.

ISBN 978-1-927583-46-3 (bound)

1. Reich, Werner—Juvenile literature. 2. Nivelli, Herbert, 1906-1977—Juvenile literature. 3. Holocaust, Jewish (1939-1945)— Juvenile literature. 4. Jewish children in the Holocaust—Biography— Juvenile literature. 5. Magicians—Germany—Biography—Juvenile literature. 6. Auschwitz (Concentration camp)—Juvenile literature.
I. Newland, Gillian, illustrator II. Title.

D804.34.K334 2014   j940.53'180922   C2014-902961-6

Editor: Kathryn Cole
Designer: Melissa Kaita

Photos on pages 28-31 courtesy Werner Reich

Printed and bound in China

Second Story Press gratefully acknowledges the support of the Ontario Arts Council, the Ontario Media Development Corporation, and the Canada Council for the Arts for our publishing program. We acknowledge the financial support of the Government of Canada through the Canada Book Fund.

Published by
SECOND STORY PRESS
20 Maud Street, Suite 401
Toronto, ON
M5V 2M5
www.secondstorypress.ca

*O*nce, there was a renowned magician called Nivelli who performed before packed audiences in the grandest theaters of Berlin. Night after night, his fans applauded and called out for more astonishing feats of magic. "Bravo!" they would shout, as Nivelli bowed low with a great flourish.

But that was in a different, happier time, before the Jews of Europe were rounded up and sent to concentration camps….

It was called the Family Camp of Auschwitz. But when Werner entered the barrack where he was to stay, he knew that this place was truly a prison. Wooden bunks lined the sides of the timber building. No pillows, no blankets, no mattresses—not even straw—cushioned the beds. Men and older boys were kept on this side of the camp. Women and young children were kept separately.

Prisoners pushed and jostled Werner on all sides as they scrambled to get a place on a lower bunk.

"I can't climb up high," an old man explained as he shoved past Werner and crawled to a spot on the lowest level of the three-tiered platform. As many as six men were crammed into each bunk.

"Only the strong will survive," another man muttered, climbing to a middle bunk.

Werner looked around, his eyes coming to rest on the third level. *I can't let anyone think I'm weak,* he thought, hoisting himself up to an empty spot.

Sitting on the edge of the highest platform was a short man with a square jaw and eyes that drooped slightly at the sides. They rested on Werner as he settled in, trying hard not to stare back at his new bunkmate. A moment later, the man held out his arm to show his number—A1676.

"We must have been on the same train," Werner said, extending his left arm. He winced slightly as he patted his new tattoo—A1828. Only one hundred and fifty-two numbers separated him from this stranger.

"My name is Levin," the man said, as he shook Werner's hand. This fellow had a soft voice, unlike the harsh bark of the guards with their growling German shepherd dogs.

"Hello, Herr Levin." Werner had always been taught by his parents to show respect to his elders, and this man was at least thirty-five, maybe even forty. He knew he must address the stranger as "mister."

"Do you have anyone else here?" the man asked.

Werner shook his head. His father had died several years earlier. The last time he had seen his mother, she was marching in the police-station courtyard where Werner had been held before being sent to the camps.

"I don't know what's happened to my older sister," Werner said, lowering his eyes. He had not seen Renate in more than two years, not since a Christian family had offered to hide her. "I hope she's all right." He reached his hand up to brush across his bare scalp; the guards had shaved the heads of all the prisoners as soon as they stumbled from the trains.

Herr Levin sighed and patted Werner's shoulder. "It's good to have hope. My wife and son are here—somewhere." He closed his eyes and took a deep breath. Werner eyed the man carefully. He seemed almost out of place here. This deadly prison was for those who were tough and could put up a good fight. Herr Levin seemed soft…gentle.

In the weeks that followed, Werner learned what life in Auschwitz was like. The days were filled with endless hours of standing in lines outside, waiting to be counted. If the count was off by even one person, the guards would start all over again, and the prisoners would have to stand even longer. Many fainted from exhaustion as the hours passed. When Werner and the others weren't waiting to be counted, the guards ordered them to do push-ups—again for hours on end. Often Werner crawled back to his bunk, wondering if he would survive another day.

The nights were just as hard. Then, Werner had his fears to keep him company.

One night, he slept restlessly. The wooden slats below him dug into his shoulders, and the blackness of night was filled with the moans of exhausted men. He finally felt himself drift off, but it seemed as if only minutes had passed before the stomping of boots filled the barracks along with voices shouting.

"Wake up! Now!"

Werner groaned, prying his eyes open. It was still pitch-black, and it took a moment for the darkened figures to come into focus. When he finally realized who these shadowy night visitors were, Werner sat straight up. Six guards stood in front of his bunk, eyes levelled on the top tier. *This is it,* Werner thought. *They've come to take me away.* He fought to calm the thumping of his heart in his chest. But Werner was not the focus of the guards' attention that night.

"You!" One of the guards pointed at Werner's bunkmate. "Get down here. Hurry!"

Herr Levin cast one look at Werner and then swung his legs over the side of the bunk and jumped to the floor. Werner's heart was still pounding. Was he about to lose the one person who had been kind to him in Auschwitz? But instead of marching his friend out the door, the guards surrounded him and ordered him to do something extraordinary.

"Do your magic!"

What was that? Magic? In Auschwitz?

Werner watched as one of the guards produced a pack of playing cards and thrust it at Herr Levin. "Show us your tricks!"

Werner peered over the side of the bunk, anxious to see what was unfolding on the floor below him. Herr Levin reached for the deck of cards and began to shuffle them. Slowly at first, and then picking up the pace, he cut the deck in half, moving the cards back and forth, in and out of the pile. Soon, he was shuffling with such skill and speed that the cards almost seemed to disappear and then materialize somewhere else—behind the ear of one of the guards, in the magician's own uniform pocket, behind another guard's back.

The guards laughed and cheered. "Another trick!" "Don't stop!" "Do that one! Again!"

Werner was spellbound. By now, other prisoners were awake. Everyone hung off their bunks, watching the magician perform his card tricks. Finally, after what felt like hours, the guards ordered Herr Levin back onto his bunk. They turned and marched out of the barracks.

Herr Levin put the pack of cards in his pocket, lay back on the wooden slats and closed his eyes. His face was pale and the lines that ran across his forehead seemed to have deepened.

"I never knew," Werner whispered. "How did you do that?"

But there was no answer. Herr Levin had fallen asleep and lay snoring softly next to Werner.

Who is this mysterious man? he wondered.

After that first time, there were many nights that Werner's sleep was interrupted. The guards would enter the barracks, stomp down the center of the building and come to a halt next to his bunk. They would order Herr Levin to wake up and perform for them. Sometimes, the magician worked with only the pack of playing cards. But soon, he began to add other tricks. He performed with coins that the guards threw to him, moving them across his fingers, and making them appear to pass through his hand as if they had turned into mist.

One night, Werner watched as the magician seemed to cut a piece of string in half with a pocketknife that he borrowed from one of the guards. He rolled the two lengths of string together into one ball. Then, he threw the ball of twine high into the air. It hung, suspended for a moment in space, and then it slowly unwound as the original un-cut string floated down, and came to rest in the magician's outstretched hand!

The guards roared their approval. Light was beginning to trickle through slits in the wooden walls of the barracks when Herr Levin finally crawled back up to the top bunk next to Werner.

"That was wonderful!" Werner exclaimed. "And the guards loved it. Perhaps you'll have an extra slice of bread to eat today."

Herr Levin eyed Werner carefully and then slowly shook his head from side to side. "You don't understand this, do you?" he asked. "And how could you?" He pulled the collar of Werner's prisoner uniform toward himself, until the two of them were eye to eye. "Listen to me. This is not a game, and it is not a show." His voice was hardly more than a whisper. "If I displease these

guards, if I fail in my magic, if I run out of tricks, if they tire of me…my life will be over." Then he lay back down and closed his eyes.

Werner fell back, his mouth open, as he took in what Herr Levin had just said. He had thought that the magician was performing his tricks simply to entertain the guards. He never realized, until that moment, that Herr Levin was performing for his life.

A week later, Werner returned to the barracks after a long day of moving rocks from one pile to another. His back and arms ached, and worse, his stomach begged for food that he knew would not come for hours. This morning had been one of the worst. The evening before, Werner had received his usual ration for supper—a bowl of watery soup with two small potato pieces, and a slice of bread made from flour and sawdust. Werner gulped the soup, as he always did, but decided he would save the bread for morning. It might help him live another day. His prison uniform already hung loosely from his body.

That night, Werner slept with the slice of bread under his head. But when he awoke in the morning, the bread was gone; someone had stolen it while he slept.

The magician was already on the bunk when Werner crawled up. He wanted to close his eyes for just a few minutes. Maybe he could forget the gnawing hunger and the feeling that there was nothing left in his life. But Herr Levin would not leave him alone.

"Don't turn away. Tell me what's wrong, my young friend." He probed and questioned until Werner finally sat up.

At first, Werner would not look at Herr Levin and hung his head low on his chest. His face looked as if it might crumple at any moment. But then, after gentle prodding, he began to tell Herr Levin about his lost rations. "It's my own fault," he cried. "I should have eaten the bread right away!"

"Yes," Herr Levin said. "You must protect what belongs to you."

"But what do I have?" Werner cried. He had come to Auschwitz with nothing and he had received nothing—just a number, a prison uniform, and barely enough food to survive. And now, a fellow inmate had taken some of that food. He didn't even have family to comfort him, just the memory of his mother's love, his father's guidance, and his sister's face. He felt worse than ever. "How is it possible that we can steal from each other?"

"It's wrong that someone took your bread," Herr Levin continued. "But here, we are all just trying to stay alive. Don't forget that."

Werner nodded. It calmed him to listen to Herr Levin. His bunkmate was wise—almost like the father he had lost so early in his life.

"Look. I have something to show you." Herr Levin reached into his pocket and pulled out the pack of dirty playing cards. Werner pushed his suffering aside. He was curious now and faced Herr Levin who fanned the cards out in front of him.

"I have a trick for you," he said. "Would you like to see it?"

Werner nodded.

"Pick a card. Don't point at it and don't tell me what it is. Just remember it."

Werner's eyes rested on the eight of spades.

"Got it?" the magician asked. Werner nodded again.

The magician shuffled the cards and then held the deck up with the bottom card facing Werner. "Is this your card?" he asked, holding up the two of diamonds.

"No," Werner replied.

Herr Levin took the card and slapped it, face down, on the wooden bunk. Then he shuffled the deck again and held up another card. It was the king of hearts. "Is this it?"

Werner shook his head. Again, the card was discarded, face down on the bunk.

For the third time, the magician shuffled the deck and held up a card—the three of clubs. "Is this it?"

And for the third time, Werner shook his head as the magician took that card and discarded it as well.

"Are you sure your card isn't amongst those three?" the magician asked, pointing to the cards that lay between them.

"I'm sure," Werner replied. *This trick isn't going very well*, he thought.

"Take a look," the magician said.

"But I know it's not there."

"Just look," the magician urged.

Werner reached for the three cast-off cards. There was the two of spades, the king of hearts, and—

What was this? The third rejected card, the one on top, was the one that Werner had picked in the first place—the eight of spades. He looked up, amazed.

"But, how did you do that?" he asked. "Where did my card come from?"

Herr Levin smiled. "A magician never reveals his secrets. But for you, I'm willing to make an exception. Would you like me to teach you how to do that trick?"

For the next hour, Herr Levin worked with Werner, teaching him the secret of the card trick. At first, Werner was clumsy; he dropped cards, and was so slow that anyone could have guessed what he was doing. But Herr Levin was a patient teacher, and soon, Werner's speed and agility increased. Before long, he was able to move and conceal the cards almost like an expert. Herr Levin nodded approvingly.

"That trick is just for you," he said. "No one else."

Werner's eyes shone, and for just a moment the misery of Auschwitz melted away. No one except the two of them could understand how special this moment was. In this dreadful place where there was nothing to own and nothing to give, the magician had given Werner a gift. It wasn't like a book or a new jacket, things that he had received in the past. It was more special.

"Magic has helped keep me alive here," Herr Levin continued. "Perhaps it will help you as well."

Werner nodded. It was nearly impossible to think about a future here. But in that moment, he felt less afraid and less alone. Someone had cared about him and given him some hope. There was enough real magic in that for Werner to hold on to.

"Thank-you," he said, after he had repeated the trick a dozen times under the watchful eyes of the magician. "I'll never forget it—or you."

And he never did.

Many years passed. Werner grew up, and what he had endured in the concentration camp became a memory that was still difficult but softened by time. He was strong and walked tall. Only those who knew him well would have detected his slight limp; a leftover from his days of cruel treatment and hard labor. He had heard that Herr Levin also had survived the camps, though the two of them had never met again since their time in Auschwitz.

One day, Werner stood on a stage in front of an audience. It wasn't a grand theater, and the people who had come to watch him were mostly friends and family members. In his hands was a shiny new pack of cards, which he shuffled, moving them back and forth with the skill and speed of an expert. The crowd gasped as the cards seemed to disappear magically, and then reappear in his other hand, and then in his pocket. Finally, he called a volunteer up to the stage and fanned the cards out in front of him. "Pick a card," he said. "Don't point at it, and don't tell me what it is. Just remember it."

When he finished the trick, the crowd applauded and cheered. "Bravo!" they shouted. Werner responded with a deep bow.

In the audience that day were two young boys who came running up to Werner as he finished his act and left the stage.

"That was great, Dad!" Michael, the youngest, spoke first. He jumped up and down and pumped his father's hand.

"Can you teach us how to do that?" Werner's oldest, David, was usually the quieter of the two, but today he was jumping and shouting as much his younger brother.

Werner paused and looked down at his sons. His gaze shifted from one eager face to the other. "A magician never reveals his secrets," he replied. Then a slow smile spread across his face. "But for you, I'm willing to make an exception."

How it Happened

Werner Reich was just a boy when he was taken from his home and sent, first to a place called Terezin, and then to the Auschwitz concentration camp. It was there, that he met a magician. Werner knew him only as Herr Levin—tattoo number A1676.

Werner's bunkmate was Herbert Levin. Before the war, Levin had been a well-regarded magician who performed in all of the best theaters of Berlin. Early in his career, Levin created his stage name. He reversed the letters in Levin, added a few, and became Nivelli the Magician. His career was cut short when he, his wife, and son were arrested and eventually sent to Auschwitz.

The magic that Nivelli performed for the guards probably saved him. And the guards promised that if he performed well enough, his family would also live. Sadly, that was not the case; Nivelli's wife and son were killed before the war ended.

The Nivellis

Werner and his sister Renate

Once, Nivelli showed Werner how to do a special card trick. He never forgot it and when he was liberated, he got hold of a deck of cards, and showed this trick to the first person he could find. That began Werner's life-long interest in magic.

Werner was eventually moved from Auschwitz to another deadly concentration camp called Mauthausen. As the war finally drew to an end and Allied troops closed in on Nazi Germany, Jewish prisoners, like Werner, were rounded up from all the concentration camps and forced on what became known as the Death March. Prisoners were marched deep into the center of Germany. Many fell from exhaustion and starvation and were left to die or were killed. Werner was among the survivors.

Werner, age 11

Werner, age 14

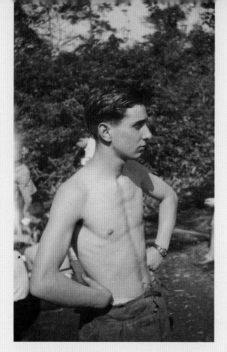

Werner was very sick when the war ended.

This certificate shows that Werner was liberated in Mauthausen.

When the war ended, he was seventeen years old, weighed only sixty-four pounds, and was very sick. After a long recovery, Werner moved to England where he married his first and only love, Eva Schiff. After a time, Werner and Eva moved to the United States. There, Werner discovered that his sister, Renate, had also survived in hiding in Italy. She too, eventually moved to the United States. Werner finally became an industrial engineer, but he never lost his interest in magic. He attended magic conventions, got to know some of the world's finest magicians, and became a member of several magicians' associations. He often performed for friends and at charity events. He and Eva now live in New York. They have two married sons who were introduced to magic at a young age, and four grandchildren.

Nivelli also survived the war, but by the time he was liberated, he was terribly ill and close to death. He managed to recover and slowly rebuilt his life, as a magician. In 1947, he too, moved to the United States and married a woman whose name was Lottie. She became his onstage assistant, and together

Werner and Eva

they traveled across the country, performing as The Nivellis.

The last performance that Nivelli gave was on May 1, 1977, in Lancaster, Pennsylvania before an audience of over fifteen hundred people. He died two days later. People who knew him said that even though he had suffered so much in his life, he remained a gentleman until the end.

Werner learned of Nivelli the Magician's death from an article in a magician's magazine. Werner didn't recognize the name, but the article also recorded the number that had been tattooed on Nivelli's arm in Auschwitz—A1676. Werner recognized that at once, and realized that this was his friend, Herr Levin, who had bunked next to him in that terrible prison, who had been kind to him when few others were, and who had once given him the gift of magic.

Werner still performs magic tricks to this day.

Werner and author, Kathy Kacer

Where it Happened

When Adolf Hitler came to power in Germany in 1933, he introduced laws and rules to limit the freedom of Jewish people. Jews could not work in their chosen professions, shop in stores, or own property. Jewish children could not go to school. Jewish people had to wear the yellow Star of David on their clothing, singling them out for discrimination. As these and many more laws were passed, Jews across Europe began to fear for their safety. Hitler vowed that he would rid the world of Europe's Jews.

Eventually, Jewish people were arrested and sent to prisons—concentration camps—that had been set up in remote areas across Europe. The conditions inside the camps were appalling. Prisoners had little food to eat, were made to do backbreaking labor, and slept in long barracks on hard wooden bunks. Many were beaten and tortured. Disease was rampant. Some camps were set up for the sole purpose of killing as many Jews as possible.

One of the worst concentration camps was the place called Auschwitz. In fact, Auschwitz was comprised of dozens of smaller camps. Some of them were for forced labor. One of them, known as Birkenau, was a death camp.

It is estimated that by the time the Second World War ended in 1945, more than six million Jews perished in what became known as the Holocaust. Of that number, at least one million Jews were killed in Auschwitz.

These children were imprisoned in Auschwitz.